The future of audiobook self-publishing: Create, Edit and Publish on Amazon Audible with the Power of AI (artificial intelligence)

Sébastien JULLIARD-BESSON - AI (Artificial Intelligence) for everyone - Digital Workout
2024

Foreword

On the threshold of a technological revolution in which artificial intelligence (AI) is redefining the contours of our daily lives, the field of audio books is moving towards an era of unprecedented transformation. Drawing on my own experience, enriched by my exploration of AI in self-publishing on Amazon KDP, I invite you to plunge into a new publishing adventure with this book. Embracing the advent of AI in audio production, this book aims to guide you through the twists and turns of innovation, ethics and marketing, into the fascinating world of AI-assisted audio books.

This exploration is intended as a bridge between my previous experiences and the future potential offered by AI, paving the way for enriched narratives and cutting-edge audio productions. Through this journey, we'll look at the technical foundations, significant developments and ethical and legal considerations, while putting into practice concrete applications of AI in audio. From content preparation to distribution, recording, sound design and intelligent marketing, this book aims to broaden your horizons and equip you to successfully navigate the new era of audio books.

Let this book be for you a source of inspiration, a practical guide and a reflection on the profound implications of AI in audio creation. Embark on this adventure, where technology and creativity meet to redefine the listening experience and open up unexplored possibilities in the audiobook world.

Sébastien JULLIARD-BESSON

Chapter 1: Understanding AI applied to audiobooks

A. Foundations of artificial intelligence in audio production

The impact of artificial intelligence on audio production is profound and revolutionary. Diving into this sub-chapter, we'll explore the inner workings of this revolution, highlighting the main pillars and key techniques shaping this evolution.

1. Introduction to audio AI

Artificial intelligence applied to audio production is based on sophisticated algorithms capable of analyzing, generating and manipulating sound data intelligently. This approach is revolutionizing the way audio content is created, distributed and consumed. We'll dive into the subtleties of this innovative approach and its transformative potential in the audiobook field.

2. Machine learning techniques

Machine learning is at the heart of audio AI. Through techniques such as deep neural networks, support vector machines (SVMs) and clustering algorithms, AI can analyze the complex structures of audio data, extract meaningful patterns and generate tailored audio content. We'll explore these techniques in detail, looking at how they're being applied to optimize audiobook production and quality.

3. Natural language processing (NLP)

Natural language processing (NLP) is an essential component of audio AI, enabling the understanding and manipulation of human language. Technologies such as speech recognition, text-to-speech and machine translation are revolutionizing the way audiobooks are created and consumed. We'll delve into the underlying mechanisms of NLP, exploring how these advances are transforming audiobook storytelling and accessibility.

B. AI developments in audio books

Artificial intelligence (AI) has travelled a fascinating path in the audiobook field, evolving from simple storytelling assistance to a real revolution in the way audio content is produced, distributed and consumed. This sub-chapter dives into the history and evolution of AI applied to audiobooks, highlighting the key milestones and advances that have shaped this constantly evolving landscape.

1. Origins of AI in audio production

An exploration of the early work and experiments that laid the foundations for AI in the audiobook field. From early attempts at speech synthesis to the first speech recognition systems, we trace the evolution of the technologies that paved the way for modern audio AI.

2. Recent advances and emerging trends

We'll dive into the recent advances that have propelled audio AI to new horizons. From more realistic voice generation algorithms to more sophisticated natural language processing models, we'll explore the technological developments that are redefining the possibilities and limits of automated audio production.

3. Impact on the audiobook industry

Examining how AI has transformed the audiobook industry, we'll highlight the major changes that have occurred in the creation, distribution and consumption of audio content. From authors to publishers, streaming platforms to online libraries, we'll analyze how AI has reshaped the entire audiobook ecosystem and redefined listeners' expectations.

C. Ethics and legal considerations related to the use of AI in audiobooks

The integration of artificial intelligence (AI) into audiobook production raises a host of important ethical and legal issues. This subchapter examines the complex issues surrounding the use of AI in audiobooks, highlighting the ethical dilemmas, legal concerns and moral considerations that accompany this technological development.

1. Accountability and transparency

One of the main ethical concerns surrounding the use of AI in audiobooks is the question of liability. Who is liable in the event of error or harm caused by AI-generated audio content? We will also address the issue of transparency and disclosure of algorithmically generated content, and how to ensure that listeners are informed about the automated nature of audio creation.

2. Copyright protection and intellectual property

The integration of AI into audiobook creation raises complex questions about copyright and intellectual property. How can we protect authors' original works and guarantee fair remuneration for their work? We will also explore the challenges of using copyrighted works in automated audio generation models.

3. Bias and algorithmic discrimination

AI systems are not immune to human bias and prejudice. In the context of audiobooks, this raises important concerns about fair representation and diversity in AI-generated content. We will analyze the measures needed to mitigate the risks of algorithmic discrimination and promote inclusive and ethical representation in AI-generated audiobooks.

STEP BY STEP IMPLEMENTATION: Exploring the basic concepts of AI for audiobooks

A. Introduction to machine learning and natural language processing algorithms

To explore the foundations of machine learning and natural language processing (NLP) in the world of audio books, here's a method enriched with concrete examples:

1. Machine learning fundamentals

Start with basic educational resources such as the online course "Machine Learning" by Andrew Ng on Coursera or the book "Deep Learning" by Ian Goodfellow, Yoshua Bengio and Aaron Courville. These resources cover the key concepts of supervised, unsupervised and reinforcement learning, as well as introductions to the main algorithms.

2. Working with datasets

Kaggle is an excellent platform for finding datasets dedicated to NLP and audio. For example, the "LibriSpeech" dataset is a large corpus of English speech that can be used for speech recognition experiments. Start with simple tasks like sentiment classification or intent detection to get used to handling this data.

3. Machine learning libraries and NLP

Python offers powerful libraries such as TensorFlow or PyTorch for machine learning, and NLTK (Natural Language Toolkit) or spaCy for NLP. For beginners, the official TensorFlow website offers tutorials for building text classification models, while spaCy offers comprehensive documentation for natural language processing, perfect for analyzing the content of audio books.

4. Practical project

To apply your knowledge, consider creating an audiobook recommendation system using the Surprise library, a Python library specialized in recommendation systems. Another interesting project could be the development of an automatic audio book summary tool using OpenAI's GPT-3, accessible via the OpenAI API, to generate relevant and captivating summaries.

5. Get involved in the community

GitHub is an essential platform for sharing your projects and learning from others. Forums like Stack Overflow and LinkedIn groups dedicated to AI and machine learning are also valuable resources for exchanging ideas and receiving advice.

6. Continuing to learn

As the field of AI is constantly evolving, it's crucial to stay informed. The "DeepMind" blog and the MIT Technology Review are good sources for keeping up with the latest developments. Conferences such as NeurIPS or ICML also offer insight into cutting-edge research and future trends.

B. Practical examples of AI applications in the generation of synthetic voices and automated narrations

The integration of artificial intelligence into synthetic voice creation and automatic narration is transforming audiobook production. Here's how to explore and apply these advances:

1. Synthetic voice generation

Google Cloud Text-to-Speech and Amazon Polly are examples of services that use AI to convert text into natural speech. These platforms offer a variety of voices and languages, enabling users to personalize the narration of their audiobooks. To get started, experiment with these services by converting an excerpt of text into speech, adjusting speed, tone, and intonation to find the style that best matches your content.

2. Creating automated narrations

Tools such as Descript and Adobe Audition offer advanced features for the automatic editing and creation of narrations. Not only can they generate speech from text, they can also edit audio recordings as if they were text. Embark on an automated narration project by importing a script into these programs and using their AI features to create a fluid and expressive narration.

3. Personalized narration

Use IBM Watson Text to Speech to experiment with personalized voices. IBM Watson lets you create unique synthetic voices from voice recordings, providing an opportunity to further personalize audiobook narration without requiring a human narrator for each book.

4. DIY (Do It Yourself) projects

For those who wish to go further, open-source projects such as Mozilla TTS provide the tools you need to build your own text-to-speech system. This requires a certain amount of technical expertise, but allows complete customization and adaptation to your specific needs.

5. Content analysis and adaptation

AI can also be used to dynamically adapt narrative content to suit the target audience. For example, platforms like Aflorithmic can create personalized audio experiences by integrating user data into the narrative, making each listen unique.

6. Learning and resources

For those wishing to deepen their knowledge of voice generation and automated narration, online courses on Udemy or Coursera, such as "AI For Everyone" by Andrew Ng, can offer a solid grounding in the use of AI in different contexts, including audio production.

By following these steps and leveraging these resources, you can not only improve the quality and accessibility of your audiobooks, but also explore new and creative ways to engage your audience.

C. Discussion of the ethical and artistic implications of using AI to create audio content

The adoption of artificial intelligence in audio content creation is sparking a debate rich in ethical and artistic implications. This exchange is essential for navigating the evolving landscape of audio production. Here are some key points to engage in this discussion:

1. Authenticity and Creativity

The use of AI to create synthetic voices and automated narratives raises questions about the authenticity of the artistic experience. What is the artistic value of a work created or interpreted by a non-human intelligence? Creative professionals need to consider how far AI should influence the creative process without compromising artistic authenticity.

2. Copyright and Intellectual Property

Who owns the rights to an AI-generated work? This complex question calls for new thinking on copyright legislation, especially for works where AI plays a significant role in creation or performance.

3. Transparency and Disclosure

It's vital to be transparent about the use of AI in content creation. Listeners need to be informed when synthetic voices are used, ensuring a clear understanding of what they are consuming.

4. Impartiality and fairness

AI is not immune to the biases present in the data on which it is trained. Creators must ensure that AI systems promote diversity and inclusion, avoiding the reproduction of stereotypes or discrimination.

5. Impact on Industry

The automation of audio storytelling and content creation by AI could redefine traditional roles in the industry, affecting jobs and the skills required. An open dialogue on how to navigate this transition is needed to balance innovation with preserving opportunities for human creators.

6. Education & Training

As AI becomes more prevalent in audio content creation, training creators in these technologies is crucial. This includes not only technical operation, but also a thorough understanding of the ethical and artistic implications.

7. Exploring New Artistic Forms

Despite the challenges, AI also opens doors to innovative art forms, enabling auditory experiences that were previously impossible. Creators can explore these new frontiers while reflecting on their ethical and cultural impact.

Engaging the artistic community, legislators, and the public in these discussions is vital to shaping a future where AI enriches audio creation without compromising fundamental ethical and artistic values. These dialogues will establish responsible practices that respect both the potential of AI and artistic integrity.

Chapter 2: Preparing content with AI

A. Using AI to adapt and select works

Artificial intelligence (AI) is revolutionizing the way works are adapted and selected for audiobook creation. This sub-chapter explores in depth the various applications of AI in this field, highlighting the methods and tools used to adapt and select works intelligently and efficiently.

1. Intelligent adaptation of the works

AI offers unique capabilities for adapting literary works to different audio formats, taking into account factors such as length, tone and narrative style. We will explore automatic text adaptation techniques, including intelligent segmentation, content reduction and expansion, and contextual adaptation for different audiences and platforms.

2. Automated selection of works

The use of AI in the selection of audio works makes it possible to identify and recommend content that is relevant and appealing to listeners. We will examine machine learning-based recommendation methods, such as user preference modeling, semantic analysis of texts and collaborative filtering, to offer personalized suggestions tailored to listeners' interests.

3. Taking preferences and trends into account

AI also makes it possible to analyze listener preferences and market trends to guide the selection of audio works. We'll cover data collection and analysis techniques, such as tracking listening behaviors, analyzing comments and ratings, and identifying emerging trends, to inform work selection and adaptation decisions.

B. AI-assisted content analysis and segmentation

The integration of artificial intelligence (AI) into the content analysis and segmentation of audio works is revolutionizing the way audiobooks are produced and structured. This sub-chapter explores in depth the methods and tools used to effectively analyze and segment audio content using AI.

1. Automatic content analysis

AI offers advanced capabilities for automatically analyzing the content of audio works, identifying themes, characters, events and sentiments expressed. We'll dive into content analysis techniques, such as semantic analysis, named entity extraction and sentiment analysis, to effectively understand and categorize audiobook content.

2. Intelligent segmentation of works

The use of AI enables audio works to be automatically segmented into meaningful units, such as chapters, scenes or thematic sections. We will explore AI-assisted segmentation methods, including the use of pre-trained language models, content break detection techniques and clustering algorithms, to create a coherent and logical structure in audiobooks.

3. Contextual adaptation and personalization

AI also makes it possible to adapt segmentation to the context and preferences of listeners, offering a personalized and immersive audio experience. We'll look at techniques for dynamically adapting segmentation, such as analyzing listener interactions, modeling user preferences and automatically adjusting narrative structure based on audience feedback.

C. Screenwriting and generative storytelling with AI

The integration of artificial intelligence (AI) into scriptwriting and generative storytelling is opening up exciting new perspectives in audiobook creation. This sub-chapter explores the methods and tools used to develop scripts and audio narratives in an automated and intelligent way thanks to AI.

1. Automatic scenario generation

AI offers unique capabilities for automatically generating narrative scenarios, taking into account elements such as characters, plots, narrative arcs and climaxes. We'll dive into AI-assisted script generation techniques, such as natural language generation models, recurrent neural networks and reinforcement learning techniques, to create captivating and original stories.

2. Automatic and expressive narration

The use of AI also enables the automatic generation of expressive and immersive audio narratives, bringing characters and events to life with natural, emotionally rich voices. We'll explore advanced text-to-speech techniques, such as convolutional neural networks and prosody models, to produce high-quality, fully personalized voice recordings.

3. Contextual and interactive adaptation

AI also makes it possible to adapt narration in real time according to the context and interactions of listeners, offering an interactive and dynamic audio experience. We'll look at techniques for adapting narration to listeners' preferences and actions, such as generating narrative variants, personalized responses to interactions, and automatic adjustments to narrative tone and style based on audience feedback.

STEP BY STEP IMPLEMENTATION: Using AI tools to select and adapt audio content

A. Exploring platforms and software offering AI capabilities for analyzing and recommending relevant audio content

In the ever-expanding world of audio books, using artificial intelligence tools to select and adapt relevant audio content is becoming common practice. Here's how to explore and use these tools:

1. Spotify for Podcasts

Spotify uses advanced AI algorithms to recommend podcasts based on users' listening habits. For audio content creators, this means that understanding how these algorithms rank and recommend content can help optimize the visibility of their own podcasts.

2. Audible by Amazon

Audible uses AI to recommend audiobooks to users, based on their previous listens and purchases. Authors and publishers can take advantage of these features by ensuring that their books are correctly tagged and described to appear in relevant recommendations.

3. Google Podcasts Manager

This tool offers detailed insights into podcast listening, enabling creators to understand how their content is discovered and consumed. Analysis of this data can help adjust content strategies to better meet audience preferences.

4. SoundCloud

Although known for its music, SoundCloud also offers a platform for podcasts, with AI-powered recommendations. This offers an opportunity for creators to reach a new, engaged audience.

5. YouTube for Audio Content

YouTube uses complex algorithms to recommend videos, including audio content such as podcasts and audiobooks. Understanding SEO on YouTube can help improve visibility and engagement.

6. Anchor

A podcasting platform that facilitates the creation, distribution and monetization of podcasts. Anchor offers detailed audience statistics, which can help refine content to better meet listeners' expectations.

7. Podbean

Podbean uses AI to recommend podcasts to listeners, and offers creators analytics tools to track the performance of their content. It's a great platform for experimenting with audio content distribution and marketing.

To take full advantage of these tools, start by creating quality content that engages your audience. Then use the analytics provided by these platforms to analyze your audience's preferences, adjust your content accordingly, and explore promotion and advertising options to reach a wider audience. The key is to stay abreast of the latest AI trends and continually adapt your strategy to make the most of the technologies available.

B. Methods for identifying and selecting text passages suitable for audio narration

Identifying and selecting text passages suitable for audio narration is crucial to creating captivating, immersive audiobooks. Here's a methodical approach that authors, editors and content creators can follow to optimize their content for audio narration:

1. Content analysis with AI

Use artificial intelligence tools to analyze the text and identify the passages that carry the most emotion or are crucial to the story. Tools like IBM Watson Natural Language Understanding can help assess emotionality and key themes in the text, enabling the selection of passages that will have a strong impact in audio narration.

2. Simplifying and adapting the text

Some written texts may require adaptation to be effectively conveyed in audio format. Use AI-based editing tools, such as Grammarly or Hemingway Editor, to simplify and clarify language, ensuring that selected passages are understandable and captivating when listened to.

3. Highlighting key dialogue and narrative elements

Strong dialogue and narrative elements are particularly effective in audio. Identify these elements in your text and consider highlighting them in audio narration. Text analysis tools can help locate these dynamic or emotionally charged passages.

4. Readability and fluidity test

Before finalizing the selection, test the readability and flow of the chosen passages using text-to-speech technologies to hear how they sound when narrated. Platforms such as Google Cloud Text-to-Speech allow you to convert text to speech with different voices and accents, offering a preview of the auditory experience.

5. Feedback from target listeners

Collect feedback from a small group of target listeners to assess the impact and clarity of selected passages. Use online survey platforms such as SurveyMonkey or Google Forms to gather feedback and adjust your selection according to your audience's preferences.

6. Optimization based on feedback

Finally, use the feedback collected to refine your selection of passages. Ongoing analysis of listener preferences can reveal specific trends and preferences, guiding future content selections for audio storytelling.

By following these steps, creators can ensure that their audio content is not only faithful to the source text but also optimized for listener engagement and immersion, thus fully exploiting the possibilities offered by audio storytelling.

C. Step-by-step tutorial for using AI algorithms to revise and enhance the initial audio script

Using artificial intelligence algorithms to edit and enhance audio scripts can transform raw text into captivating, polished narration. Here's a step-by-step method for applying AI in this process:

1. Preparing the initial script

- Start with a raw script that has been written or selected for audio narration.
- Make sure the text is complete and ready for initial processing by the AI.

2. Script analysis with AI

- Use AI-based text analysis tools, such as Grammarly or Hemingway, to identify grammatical errors, complex sentences and suggestions for stylistic improvement.
- Apply the corrections recommended by these tools to improve text clarity and readability.

3. Enriching the script with narrative elements

Integrate AI tools like OpenAI's GPT to suggest additions or modifications that enrich the story, add depth to the characters, or improve the flow of the narrative.

4. Personalizing narration with AI

 - For scripts aimed at specific audiences or genres, use AI tools to adapt tone, style and vocabulary. Platforms like IBM Watson can help analyze and adjust the script according to listeners' anticipated listening preferences.

5. Text-to-speech (TTS)

- Convert the enhanced script into audio using a high-quality text-to-speech service such as Google Cloud Text-to-Speech or Amazon Polly.
- Choose a voice that matches the tone of the story, and test different parameters to get the most natural rendering possible.

6. Review and feedback

- Listen to the generated audio and note the sections that could benefit from further improvement, whether in terms of vocal performance or script content.
- Repeat the process of analysis and improvement with AI tools to refine the script and narrative.

7. Implementation of auditor feedback

- After the initial publication, collect feedback from auditors to identify areas for improvement.
- Use AI to analyze comments and adjust the script accordingly for future narrations.

8. Finalization

- Once you're happy with the result, finalize the audio version of the script.
- Consider using AI tools to distribute and recommend finished audio content, maximizing its impact and reach.

This process illustrates how integrating AI into the revision and enhancement of audio scripts can not only improve the quality of narrative content, but also personalize the listening experience to meet the specific expectations of listeners.

Chapter 3: AI-assisted recording and production

A. AI-based audio recording and processing tools

In the field of audio recording and production, artificial intelligence (AI) offers revolutionary tools to improve the quality, efficiency and creativity of the creative process. This sub-chapter explores the various AI-based tools and techniques used for audio recording and processing.

1. Improved audio quality

AI tools offer advanced features to improve the audio quality of recordings, reducing background noise, eliminating unwanted artifacts and optimizing sound clarity and sharpness. We'll explore machine learning-based noise removal techniques, audio restoration algorithms and distortion reduction models to ensure optimum audio quality.

2. Automatic editing and post-production

AI makes it possible to automate many audio editing and post-production tasks, speeding up the processing process and delivering accurate, consistent results. We'll discuss AI-assisted editing tools, such as automatic cut point detection, automatic volume normalization and automatic track synchronization, to simplify and streamline the post-production workflow.

3. AI-assisted creativity and composition

Finally, AI also offers innovative possibilities for music composition and sound design, providing tools for music generation and sound creation based on predictive models and machine learning algorithms. We will explore AI-assisted music generation techniques, harmonic and melodic composition tools, and soundscape creation systems to inspire the creativity of audio artists.

B. AI enhances sound quality and voice performance

Artificial intelligence (AI) is revolutionizing the improvement of sound quality and vocal performance in audio production. This sub-chapter explores AI-based tools and techniques used to optimize the sound quality and vocal performance of audio recordings.

1. Improved sound quality

AI tools offer advanced features to improve the sound quality of recordings, removing unwanted noise, mitigating distortion and balancing audio levels. We'll look at machine learning-based sound restoration techniques, adaptive noise removal algorithms and phase correction filters to ensure optimum sound quality.

2. Optimizing voice performance

AI makes it possible to optimize the vocal performance of audio recordings by automatically adjusting the tone, timbre and intonation of the voice. We will discuss AI-based voice enhancement tools such as real-time voice processors, automatic pitch correctors and voice modulation systems to ensure accurate and expressive vocal performance.

3. Personalization and contextual adaptation

Finally, AI offers possibilities for customization and contextual adaptation of sound quality and voice performance according to listeners' needs and preferences. We will explore automatic sound quality adaptation techniques, such as real-time dynamic adjustment of audio parameters and listening preference modeling, to deliver a tailored and immersive audio experience.

C. Automating post-production tasks with AI algorithms

The automation of audio post-production tasks using artificial intelligence (AI) represents a major advance in the efficiency and accuracy of the audio production process. This sub-chapter explores the various AI-based algorithms and techniques used to automate audio post-production tasks.

1. Automatic cleaning and restoration

AI algorithms can automatically detect and remove unwanted audio artifacts, such as clicks, pops, hiss and sibilance. We'll look at machine-learning-based automatic cleaning and restoration techniques, such as convolutional neural networks and denoising models, to ensure optimal audio quality after recording.

2. Automatic equalization and balancing

AI offers advanced features for automatically equalizing and balancing frequency and intensity levels in audio recordings. We'll look at automatic equalization algorithms based on predictive models and machine-learning techniques, such as adaptive equalization and spectral balancing, to create an even, pleasing sound balance.

3. Automated mixing and mastering

Finally, AI makes it possible to automate many stages of the audio mixing and mastering process, automatically adjusting levels, pans and sound effects to create the optimum final sound. We will explore AI-based automated mixing and mastering techniques, such as the use of neural networks for mix optimization, preset recommendation systems and automatic normalization tools to guarantee professional sound quality.

STEP-BY-STEP APPLICATION: Recording and processing audio with AI

A. AI-based audio recording and processing tools

The integration of artificial intelligence (AI) into audio recording and processing offers revolutionary tools that significantly improve the quality, efficiency and creativity of audio productions. Here's a detailed overview of AI-based tools and techniques used in this field:

1. Improved audio quality with AI

Tools like iZotope RX and Adobe Audition offer advanced features to improve audio quality, reducing background noise and eliminating unwanted artifacts. These programs use machine-learning algorithms to detect and repair sound problems intuitively and efficiently.

2. Automatic editing and post-production

AI enables many editing and post-production tasks to be automated, such as cut point detection, automatic volume normalization and track synchronization. Tools like Descript offer automated audio editing capabilities, enabling recordings to be cut, merged and cleaned up with remarkable ease.

3. AI-assisted creativity and composition

For composers and sound designers, platforms like AIVA and Amper Music use AI to generate music and sound effects. These tools make it possible to create unique compositions, based on specific styles and moods, without requiring advanced music composition skills.

4. Improved sound quality and vocal performance

AI plays a crucial role in optimizing vocal performance and the sound quality of recordings. It automatically adjusts tone, timbre and intonation to produce a natural, expressive voice. Voysis and Modulate.ai are examples of technologies that offer AI-based voice enhancement capabilities.

5. Personalization and contextual adaptation

AI also offers the ability to personalize and adapt sound quality and voice performance according to listening context and user preferences. This includes dynamic adjustment of audio parameters in real time to deliver a tailor-made listening experience.

6. Automation of post-production tasks

Automating audio post-production tasks, such as automatic cleanup and restoration, equalization and level balancing, is made simple by AI. Advanced algorithms detect and remove audio defects, guaranteeing optimum sound quality.

By adopting these AI-based tools and techniques, audio creators can not only improve the quality of their productions, but also explore new creative avenues with greater efficiency. These innovations pave the way for immersive, personalized audio experiences, redefining audio industry standards.

B. Microphone and audio interface configuration for optimum recording quality

When it comes to recording audio content, whether for audiobooks, podcasts or music, the crucial first step is to ensure that the equipment is correctly configured to capture the sound in the best possible quality. Here's a step-by-step guide to setting up your microphones and audio interfaces:

1. Microphone selection

1) *Condenser microphones*
Ideal for recording studios because of their high sensitivity and ability to capture fine detail and a wide range of frequencies. Perfect for voice and acoustic instruments.

2) *Dynamic microphones*
More robust and less sensitive to background noise, these microphones are excellent for recording live or in less controlled environments.

2. Microphone positioning

- Position the microphone at the optimum distance from the sound source, generally between 15 and 30 centimetres for voice.
- Use microphone stands and pop filters to reduce vibrations and unwanted noises, such as plosives ("p", "t", and "k").

3. Choice of audio interface

- Select a quality audio interface that can convert analog signals to digital without loss of quality. Look for interfaces with high-quality preamps and low background noise.

- Make sure the interface is compatible with your computer and recording software.

4. Software configuration

- Install the necessary drivers for your audio interface and make sure it is correctly recognized by your computer.
- Configure your recording software to use the audio interface as the main input. Adjust buffer settings to minimize latency without overloading your computer's processor.

5. Gain and level settings

- Adjust the gain levels on the audio interface to obtain a clear, distortion-free signal. The signal level should be strong, but never reach red on the meter.
- Perform recording tests to ensure that levels are constant and sound quality is at its best.

6. Monitoring and listening

- Use studio-quality headphones to monitor the recording in real time. This allows you to identify and correct sound quality problems immediately.
- Listen to the recording on different sound systems to ensure that the quality remains constant on different playback devices.

By following these steps, you'll be able to configure your equipment for optimum recording quality, laying a solid foundation for further sound processing and enhancement with artificial intelligence.

C. AI enhances sound quality and voice performance

The integration of artificial intelligence (AI) into audio production has revolutionized the improvement of sound quality and vocal performance. Here's how AI-based tools and techniques are being used to optimize audio recordings:

1. Improved sound quality

1) *Noise reduction*
Software such as iZotope RX uses AI to identify and eliminate unwanted background noise, such as hiss, clicks, or traffic noise, providing a clear, distraction-free recording.

2) *Audio restoration*
AI restores damaged or poor-quality recordings, repairing audio defects such as distortion, saturation or clipping.

3) *Automatic equalization*
AI-based tools analyze the sound spectrum and automatically adjust frequency levels to balance the audio mix and improve recording clarity.

2. Optimizing voice performance

1) *Tone correction*
AI can adjust voice pitch in vocal recordings to correct false notes or harmonize voices in a virtual choir.

2) *Improved vocal clarity*
Advanced algorithms analyze and improve diction and speech clarity, making voices more understandable and pleasant to listen to.

3) *Voice modulation*
AI can modify voice timbre and style, offering the possibility of creating customized synthetic voices or imitating specific accents for more engaging narration.

3. Personalization and contextual adaptation

1) *Dynamic adaptation*
AI can adjust audio parameters according to the listening context, such as reducing background noise in a noisy environment or adapting the mix for headphones versus speakers.

2) *Personalized audio experiences*
AI makes it possible to create personalized listening experiences, adjusting audio content to the listener's preferences in real time.

4. Practical implementation

1) *Choose the right tool*
Select AI-based audio processing software tailored to your specific needs, taking into account ease of use, features offered and cost.

2) *Analyze your audio*
Use the tool to analyze the initial recording and identify areas for improvement.

3) *Apply corrections*
Follow the tool's recommendations to apply corrections and enhancements, manually adjusting parameters if necessary to achieve the desired result.

4) *Listen and adjust*
Listen carefully to the improved recording and adjust the settings until you are satisfied with the sound quality and vocal performance.

5) *Test in different environments*
Make sure the recording sounds good in a variety of listening contexts, such as headphones, car speakers, and home audio systems.

D. Use of AI tools for sound enhancement and background noise suppression during recording

The adoption of artificial intelligence (AI) tools for audio enhancement and background noise suppression marks a significant evolution in audio recording. These technologies not only produce recordings of exceptional clarity, but also optimize post-production processes. Here's a step-by-step approach to harnessing these AI tools:

1. Selection of specialized tools

1) *iZotope RX*
Renowned for its advanced noise reduction capabilities, iZotope RX uses AI to identify and eliminate background noise, clicks and hiss without altering the quality of the main voice.

2) *Adobe Audition*
With its adaptive noise reduction features, Adobe Audition cleans up recordings by automatically adjusting settings to remove various types of background noise.

2. Preparing for recording

- Before you start recording, test your equipment to ensure that it is correctly configured and that the recording environment is as quiet as possible.
- Use directional microphones to minimize the capture of ambient noise.

3. Initial registration

Record your audio, taking care to capture the clearest, cleanest sound possible as a basis for AI enhancement.

4. Analysis and initial treatment

- Import the recording into your chosen software (iZotope RX, Adobe Audition, or other) and use the analysis tool to identify sections requiring special attention.
- Apply the audio enhancement and noise suppression features offered by the software to clean up your recording. These tools automatically adjust parameters based on AI analysis to optimize sound quality.

5. Fine-tuning and customization

Listen carefully to the processed recording and manually adjust the parameters if necessary to achieve the best result. The aim is to eliminate background noise without compromising the quality of the voice or main instrument.

6. Validation and further adjustments

After applying the initial improvements, it may be useful to submit the recording to a small group of listeners for feedback. Use their comments to make further adjustments if necessary.

7. Integration into the final project

- Once you're happy with the result, integrate the enhanced recording into your final audio project, whether it's an audiobook, podcast or music production.

8. Preservation of original versions

It's always a good idea to keep a copy of the original recording. In the event of over-processing, or if future adjustments are necessary, you will always have access to the unaltered source.

E. AI-assisted audio post-production techniques for mixing, equalization and correction of vocal imperfections

Audio post-production is a crucial stage in the production of audio content, enabling recordings to be adjusted, mixed and finalized to achieve optimum sound quality. Integrating artificial intelligence (AI) into this process opens up new possibilities for refining and perfecting audio productions with greater precision and efficiency. Here's how AI can be used for mixing, equalization and correction of vocal imperfections:

1. Automatic cleaning and restoration

1) AI algorithms for noise suppression
Use tools like iZotope RX, which employ AI to detect and eliminate background noise, clicks, pops and hiss. These tools analyze the audio file to identify sections containing unwanted noise and remove them without affecting the quality of the voice or music.

2) Restoring damaged recordings
AI can also restore poor-quality audio recordings, repairing distortion, saturation or clipping, thanks to advanced sound modeling techniques.

2. Automatic equalization and balancing

1) AI frequency adjustment

Platforms like LANDR use AI to analyze and adjust the frequency levels of audio recordings. By identifying the specific needs of each track, AI can apply precise equalization to balance the mix and improve sound clarity.

2) Optimizing audio mixing

AI can automatically adjust relative track volumes, pans and effects to create a harmonious, professional mix, taking into account industry standards and stylistic preferences.

3. Correction of vocal imperfections

1) Tone and timing correction

AI-based tools such as Celemony Melodyne correct false notes and timing problems in vocal recordings. The AI analyzes the vocal performance and suggests adjustments to improve pitch and rhythm.

2) Improved vocal clarity

AI can also process the voice to improve clarity and presence, reducing sibilance and accentuating important articulations, making narration more understandable and pleasant to listen to.

4. Personalization and contextual adaptation

1) Dynamic audio adaptation

AI can adjust the mix and audio parameters according to the broadcast context (such as switching between headphones and speakers) and the listener's preferences, offering a personalized, optimized listening experience.

5. Practical implementation

1) *Initial assessment*
Analyze the recording with an AI tool to identify areas requiring intervention.

2) *Applying corrections*
Use the tool's recommendations to automatically apply cleaning, equalization and mixing corrections.

3) *Manual adjustments*
Although AI can provide a solid foundation, manual adjustments by an experienced sound engineer may be necessary to fine-tune the final result.

4) *Testing and validation*
Listen to the final mix in different environments and with different equipment to ensure that the sound is optimal in different contexts.

Chapter 4: Sound design and AI-generated music

A. Creating sound design and music with AI

The integration of artificial intelligence (AI) into sound design and music creation is opening up new creative and innovative perspectives in audio production. This sub-chapter explores the various AI-based methods and techniques used to generate sound design and music in an automated and intelligent way.

1. Automatic sound design generation

AI tools offer advanced features to automatically generate sound design for various applications, such as film, video games and interactive media. We'll dive into sound synthesis techniques based on machine learning, adversarial generative neural networks (ANNs) and sound generation models to create immersive, evocative soundscapes.

2. AI-assisted music composition

AI can also be used to automatically compose original music to accompany audiovisual productions. We'll look at AI-assisted music composition tools, such as genetic algorithms, recurrent neural networks and melody generation models, to create unique musical compositions tailored to each project.

3. Personalization and contextual adaptation

Finally, AI offers possibilities for customization and contextual adaptation of sound design and music according to the needs and preferences of creators and users. We'll explore techniques for modeling listening preferences, sound recommendation systems and automatic personalization tools to deliver a customized, immersive audio experience.

B. Exploring AI-generated sound banks and music libraries for audiobook enrichment

The integration of artificial intelligence (AI) in the creation of sound banks and music libraries opens up new possibilities for enriching audiobooks with immersive and evocative audio elements. This sub-chapter explores the different methods and techniques used to explore and exploit these AI-generated audio resources.

1. Automatic sound bank generation

AI algorithms make it possible to automatically generate diverse sound banks suited to different genres and moods. We'll dive into sound bank generation techniques based on machine learning, audio classification models and convolutional neural networks to create rich and varied collections of ambient sounds, sound effects and audio textures.

2. Creating custom music libraries

AI also offers opportunities to create personalized music libraries to accompany audiobooks with musical compositions tailored to each project. We'll look at techniques for generating music libraries based on listening preference models, music recommendation systems and automatic composition tools to offer a varied and relevant selection of music.

3. Integration and use in audio books

Finally, we will explore methods for integrating and exploiting these soundbanks and music libraries in audiobooks, using them to enrich listeners' auditory experience and enhance narrative immersion. We'll look at audio synchronization techniques, mixing and post-production tools, and sound narration strategies to take full advantage of these AI-generated audio resources.

C. Methods for integrating sound effects and dynamic soundscapes into audio narration

The integration of sound effects and dynamic soundscapes into audio narration is an essential dimension in creating immersive and captivating aural experiences. This sub-chapter explores the various methods and techniques used to effectively and creatively integrate these audio elements into audiobooks.

1. Selection and creation of relevant sound effects

Sound effects are selected or created to enhance narrative immersion and add depth to the events described in the audiobook. We'll dive into methods for selecting suitable sound effects, creating custom sounds and using sound editing tools to ensure that sound effects integrate seamlessly with the narrative.

2. Dynamic and spatialized audio

The addition of dynamic soundscapes helps to create an enveloping and realistic atmosphere, simulating the sound environment in which the narrated events take place. We'll look at audio spatialization techniques, such as the use of binaural mixes and reverberation effects, as well as strategies for modulating sound intensity and density to create immersive, evocative atmospheres.

3. Synchronization with narration and narrated events

Integrating sound effects and soundscapes into audio narration requires precise synchronization with narrated events and narrative fluctuations. We'll look at methods of time synchronization, techniques for smooth transitions between soundscapes and sound effects, and strategies for modulating as the narrative evolves to create a coherent and engaging audio experience.

STEP BY STEP IMPLEMENTATION: Creating sound design and music with AI

A. Exploring AI tools for creating sound design and original music

The rise of artificial intelligence (AI) in music creation and sound design is opening up new avenues for composers, sound designers, and audio content creators. Here's a step-by-step approach to exploring and using these innovative tools:

1. Discover AI-based music creation platforms

1) AIVA
A platform that uses AI to compose music for films, video games and commercials. AIVA analyzes the music of great composers to create original works.

2) Amper Music
Allows users to quickly and easily create original music by specifying a few parameters such as style, tempo and duration.

2. Using AI-assisted sound design tools

1) LANDR
Offers automated mastering services using AI to analyze and optimize your audio tracks.

2) Sonic Pi
Although primarily a learning tool, Sonic Pi can be used to program live music with the support of intelligent algorithms.

3. Experimenting with AI-based plug-ins and effects

1) iZotope Ozone
Use AI for audio mastering, offering suggestions and automatic adjustments to improve the quality of your mixes.

2) Boomy
Instantly create original songs in just a few clicks, with the option of customizing AI-generated tracks.

4. Explore AI-generated sound and music libraries

Search for libraries that use AI to generate unique sounds and loops. These resources can be used to enrich your compositions or sound designs with original elements.

5. Collaboration with AI tools for music composition

Get involved in projects where AI and human creativity meet. Use AI as a tool to extend your creativity, generating ideas, melodies or rhythms that can serve as the basis for your compositions.

6. Adaptation and customization

Use AI to adapt your music and sound designs to the specific needs of your project, modifying the generated compositions to match the desired mood or theme.

7. Assessment and adjustment

Listen to and evaluate the AI's creations, and make the necessary adjustments to refine the final result. The aim is to find the right balance between the innovation provided by the AI and your artistic vision.

By integrating these AI tools into your creative process, you can push the boundaries of music creation and sound design, explore new sonic territories, and produce original, captivating works.

B. Methods for selecting and integrating sound and musical elements in audio production

The effective integration of sound and music elements greatly enriches audio productions, making them more immersive and captivating. Here's a step-by-step guide to selecting and integrating these elements into your audio projects:

1. Selecting sound and music elements

1) Content analysis
Evaluate the audio content to determine the types of sound and musical elements that will best complement the story or message. Consider the tone, rhythm and overall mood of the project.

2) Search for resources
Use sound and music libraries, including those generated by AI, to find suitable elements. Platforms such as Epidemic Sound, Artlist and AIVA offer a wide range of choices.

2. Adaptation and customization

1) *Personalization with AI*

Tools like Jukedeck (if still available) or AI-based platforms allow you to create music tailored to your specific needs. You can specify genre, tempo and even mood for original compositions.

2) *Editing and modifying*

Adjust selected elements so that they align perfectly with the audio content. This may involve trimming, fading in/out, or adjusting tempo.

3. Integration into audio production

1) *Synchronization*

Align sound and musical elements with narrative content to reinforce emotional impact or highlight key moments.

2) *Mixing*

Balance audio levels so that music and sound effects complement the narrative without overpowering it. Use mixing software to adjust levels, equalization and other parameters.

4. Assessment and adjustment

1) *Feedback*

Gather feedback on the integrated version to assess the effectiveness of sound and music integration.

2) *AI-based adjustments*

Use AI-based analysis tools to assess the impact of sound elements on the audience. Platforms like Landr can offer insights into how adjustments can improve overall quality.

5. Finalization

1) *Final validation*

Make sure that all the elements are properly integrated and that the final product is coherent and polished.

2) *Export*

Export the audio project in the desired format, taking care to maintain the highest possible quality for distribution.

This methodical approach, supported by the use of AI tools for the selection, personalization and integration of sound and musical elements, optimizes the emotional impact and audience engagement of audio productions.

C. Tutorial for personalizing the hearing experience using AI algorithms

Personalizing the auditory experience with AI algorithms makes it possible to create tailor-made listening experiences that adapt to each listener's preferences and listening contexts. Here's how it works:

1. Analysis of auditor preferences

- Collect data on listener preferences through direct interactions, listening histories or questionnaires.
- Use AI to analyze this data and identify specific patterns or preferences in terms of genres, artists, tempos and so on.

2. Selection of suitable content

- Develop or use pre-existing AI algorithms to recommend audio content based on preference analysis.
- For music, explore services like Spotify API, which offers listening-based recommendation features. For sound design, use AI tools that can generate or suggest appropriate sound effects and moods.

3. Dynamic content adaptation

- Integrate AI functionalities that adjust content in real time according to the listening context (for example, modifying volume or tempo according to the user's activity).
- Use technologies like neural networks to subtly modify music or sound design without compromising artistic quality.

4. Continuous feedback integration

- Implement a feedback system allowing users to rate their listening experience or modify their preferences.
- Regularly analyze this feedback to refine and improve recommendation and personalization algorithms.

5. Development of an intuitive user interface

- Design a user interface that allows listeners to easily indicate their preferences and control their listening experience.
- Include options for users to discover new content or modify personalization settings.

6. Testing and optimization

- Carry out tests with a varied group of listeners to evaluate the effectiveness of personalization algorithms.
- Use the data collected to optimize algorithms, improving the accuracy of recommendations and matching content to listeners' preferences.

7. Privacy and data security

Ensure that all data collected and analyzed complies with privacy laws and is secure against unauthorized access.

By following these steps, you can create an enriching personalized auditory experience, using AI to tailor audio content to the specific tastes and needs of each listener, delivering a more immersive and satisfying experience.

Chapter 5: Intelligent distribution and marketing

A. AI-based market analysis and recommendations

Integrating artificial intelligence (AI) into market analysis and recommendations offers significant benefits for audiobook distribution and marketing strategies. This sub-chapter explores the different methods and techniques used to analyze the market and formulate AI-based strategic recommendations.

1. Data analysis and market segmentation

AI algorithms can analyze large amounts of data to identify market trends, consumer behaviors and relevant market segments. We'll dive into data analysis methods, such as supervised and unsupervised machine learning, clustering and classification techniques, to segment the market and identify growth opportunities.

2. Forecasting demand and trends

AI offers advanced functionalities for forecasting future demand and anticipating market trends. We will discuss predictive modeling techniques, such as recurrent neural networks, time series methods and demand forecasting algorithms, to anticipate consumer needs and optimize distribution and marketing decisions.

3. Personalized, targeted recommendations

Finally, AI enables personalized, targeted recommendations for marketing and distribution campaigns, based on consumer preferences and behaviors. We will explore recommendation techniques based on collaborative filtering, hybrid recommendation systems and contextual recommendation models to deliver a personalized experience to listeners and maximize the effectiveness of marketing efforts.

B. Targeted promotional strategies thanks to AI

The integration of artificial intelligence (AI) into promotion strategies offers opportunities for precise targeting and personalization of marketing campaigns for audiobooks. This sub-chapter explores the different methods and techniques used to develop effective AI-based promotion strategies.

1. Advanced audience analysis

AI algorithms enable in-depth analysis of the demographics, buying behaviors and preferences of potential listeners. We'll dive into advanced audience analysis methods, such as natural language processing, supervised and unsupervised machine learning, to identify relevant audience segments and understand their specific needs.

2. Personalized messages and offers

AI offers functionalities for personalizing promotional messages and offers according to listeners' individual characteristics and preferences. We'll look at dynamic content personalization techniques, product recommendation systems and purchase propensity scoring models to deliver relevant and appealing offers to each listener.

3. Optimizing promotional channels

Finally, AI enables the optimization of promotional channels by identifying the most effective channels for reaching target audience segments. We'll explore marketing attribution modeling techniques, advertising campaign optimization algorithms and multi-channel targeting strategies to maximize the ROI of promotional efforts.

C. Optimizing advertising campaigns and visibility with AI tools

Integrating artificial intelligence (AI) into advertising campaign optimization offers opportunities to improve visibility and promotional effectiveness for audiobooks. This sub-chapter explores the various methods and techniques used to optimize advertising campaigns and increase visibility through AI.

1. Analysis and optimization of advertising performance

AI algorithms enable real-time analysis of ad campaign performance and identify the most effective strategies for achieving visibility and conversion goals. We'll dive into real-time data analysis methods, ad performance scoring models and bid optimization algorithms to maximize ad campaign ROI.

2. Personalized ads and content

AI offers features to personalize advertisements and promotional content based on the characteristics and behaviors of potential listeners. We'll look at behavioral targeting techniques, dynamic segmentation models and content recommendation systems to create relevant, engaging ads that capture listeners' attention.

3. Using machine learning to optimize campaigns

Finally, AI makes it possible to use machine learning techniques to proactively optimize advertising campaigns and improve audiobook visibility. We will explore machine learning-based optimization methods, such as closed-loop machine learning, genetic algorithms and deep neural networks, to automatically adjust campaign parameters and maximize their impact.

STEP BY STEP IMPLEMENTATION: Planning and executing an AI-based marketing strategy

A. Analysis of market data and identification of target audience segments using AI tools

The integration of artificial intelligence (AI) into market analysis and audience segmentation offers significant advantages for audiobook marketing strategies. Here's a detailed approach to harnessing these tools:

1. Market Data Collection and Analysis

Use AI tools to collect and analyze a wide variety of market data, including consumer trends, buying behaviors, and listener preferences. Platforms like Google Analytics, SEMrush, or specialized AI tools can provide valuable insights into the listening habits and interests of your target audience.

2. Audience Segment Identification

Apply machine learning techniques, such as clustering or classification, to segment the audience into distinct groups based on defined criteria (age, preferences, listening habits, etc.). Tools like IBM Watson or TensorFlow can help identify audience segments with specific needs and behaviors.

3. Customizing Marketing Strategies

Use the insights gained to personalize your marketing and content strategies. AI enables you to develop personalized recommendations, tailor marketing messages, and effectively target each audience segment with campaigns tailored to their preferences.

4. Trend and Demand Forecasting

Use predictive models to anticipate future market trends and listener demand. This enables you to adjust your audiobook offering accordingly, developing titles that meet emerging listener expectations.

5. Continuous Optimization

Integrate a continuous improvement process by regularly using AI to analyze the performance of your campaigns and the reception of your audiobooks. This helps refine audience segments, adjust marketing strategies, and respond more precisely to listeners' needs.

6. Campaign Effectiveness Evaluation

Analyze the effectiveness of your marketing campaigns by using AI tools to track conversions, engagement, and return on investment (ROI). This enables you to identify the most effective strategies and allocate resources more efficiently.

7. Confidentiality and Data Ethics

Ensure that all data collected and analyzed respects user privacy and complies with current regulations, such as the RGPD. Use AI tools that guarantee data security and confidentiality.

By following these steps, you can leverage AI to thoroughly analyze market data, precisely identify target audience segments, and customize your marketing strategies to optimize the reach and effectiveness of your audiobooks.

B. Development of personalized promotional content tailored to the preferences of potential listeners

Creating personalized promotional content that resonates with the preferences of potential listeners is crucial to the success of marketing strategies in the audiobook industry. Here's a methodical approach to developing such content using artificial intelligence (AI):

1. Analyzing Audience Data with AI

Use AI tools to analyze data collected on distribution platforms and direct feedback from listeners. Platforms like Google Analytics, combined with specific AI tools, can reveal insights into the preferences, interests and listening behaviors of target audiences.

2. AI-based Audience Segmentation

Apply machine learning algorithms to segment the audience into specific groups based on their demographics, interests and listening habits. This segmentation allows you to create tailored promotional messages that resonate with each segment.

3. Custom Content Creation

- Develop promotional content tailored to each identified audience segment. This can include personalized visuals, targeted messages, and specific offers designed to attract attention and generate interest.
- Use tools like Persado to generate AI-optimized promotional copy that increases engagement and conversion by leveraging the linguistic nuances that resonate best with your audience.

4. AI-assisted A/B testing

Set up A/B tests to evaluate the effectiveness of different promotional content with similar audience segments. Use AI to analyze results and identify the most effective approaches in terms of engagement and conversion.

5. Continuous Optimization

Integrate feedback from A/B tests and promotional campaigns to continuously refine your content strategies. AI tools can help detect patterns in performance data, enabling rapid, evidence-based adjustments.

6. Real-time personalization

Implement AI solutions capable of personalizing promotional experiences in real time, tailoring audiobook recommendations and marketing messages to user interactions on digital platforms.

7. Confidentiality

Ensure that any use of data for content personalization complies with privacy laws and regulations, giving users clear control over their data.

By following this approach, you can develop promotional content that not only captures the attention of potential listeners, but also builds commitment and loyalty to your audiobook brand, creating a truly personalized and relevant experience for each listener.

C. Use of AI algorithms to optimize advertising campaigns and dynamically adjust marketing strategies in real time

The use of artificial intelligence (AI) algorithms to optimize advertising campaigns and dynamically adjust marketing strategies in real time represents a significant advance for the audiobook sector. Here's a detailed approach to exploiting these technologies:

1. Advertising Performance Analysis and Optimization

1) Real Time Assessment
Use AI to analyze ad campaign performance in real time, enabling rapid identification of the most effective strategies for achieving visibility and conversion goals.

2) Auction Optimization
AI algorithms can automatically adjust bids for keywords or audience segments, maximizing the ROI of advertising campaigns.

2. Personalizing Ads and Content

1) *Behavioral targeting*
Leverage AI to refine behavioral targeting, creating personalized ads that resonate with the interests and behaviors of potential listeners.

2) *Dynamic Segmentation*
AI models facilitate dynamic audience segmentation, enabling more targeted and relevant advertising campaigns.

3. Campaign Optimization with Machine Learning

1) *Closed Loop Machine Learning*
Implement machine learning systems that continuously adjust and optimize campaigns based on performance, user feedback and changes in market trends.

2) *Real-time adjustments*
AI algorithms enable campaign parameters to be adjusted in real time, in response to insights generated by user performance and engagement data.

4. Putting it into practice

1) *Integration of AI Tools*
Select and integrate AI tools designed for advertising data analysis and campaign optimization into your marketing technology stack.

2) *Team training*
Make sure your marketing teams are trained to use these AI tools effectively, understand the insights generated, and make informed data-driven decisions.

3) *Continuous Testing and Evaluation*
Implement an A/B testing process to evaluate the effectiveness of different AI-optimized advertising approaches, and use the results to continuously refine your campaigns.

4) Monitoring and analysis

Use dashboards and analytics to track campaign performance and the effectiveness of adjustments made by AI, enabling rapid, data-driven decision-making.

By harnessing the capabilities of AI algorithms to optimize advertising campaigns and dynamically adjust marketing strategies, audiobook publishers and distributors can not only improve the visibility and effectiveness of their promotions, but also proactively adapt to market changes and listener preferences, ensuring a more responsive, data-driven marketing approach.

Chapter 6: AI-assisted rights management and legal aspects

A. Using AI to manage copyright and licenses

The integration of artificial intelligence (AI) into copyright and licensing management offers opportunities to automate and optimize legal processes for audiobooks. This sub-chapter explores the different methods and techniques used to effectively manage copyright and licensing using AI.

1. Automated copyright analysis

AI algorithms can automatically analyze copyrights and license agreements to identify relevant clauses and conditions. We'll dive into legal text analysis methods, pattern recognition techniques and classification models to automate copyright management and ensure compliance with contractual obligations.

2. License and royalty management

AI offers advanced functionalities for managing licenses and calculating royalties efficiently and transparently. We'll look at techniques for modeling license agreements, rights-of-use tracking systems and royalty calculation algorithms to simplify rights management processes and ensure fair remuneration for creators and rights holders.

3. Detecting and preventing rights violations

Finally, AI can detect and prevent copyright infringement by actively monitoring the use of protected content and identifying potential infringements. We will explore methods for monitoring content use, similarity detection algorithms and early warning systems to protect creators' rights and take remedial action in the event of infringement.

B. Automated control of compliance with standards and regulations

The integration of artificial intelligence (AI) into automated standards and regulations compliance monitoring offers opportunities to ensure legal and regulatory compliance of audiobooks in an efficient and proactive way. This sub-chapter explores the various methods and techniques used to monitor compliance with standards and regulations using AI.

1. Automated regulatory analysis

AI algorithms automatically analyze regulations and standards applicable to audiobooks to identify relevant requirements and obligations. We'll dive into legal text analysis methods, regulatory modeling techniques and regulatory update monitoring systems to ensure ongoing compliance with current standards.

2. Verification of content and practices

AI offers advanced functionalities for automatically checking the compliance of content and practices with current standards and regulations. We'll look at natural language processing techniques, content classification models and anomaly detection systems to identify deviations from standards and take timely corrective action.

3. Continuous monitoring and preventive alerts

Finally, AI can be used to continuously monitor compliance with standards and regulations, and issue preventive alerts in the event of potential non-compliance. We will explore methods for monitoring business practices, irregularity detection algorithms and real-time alert systems to ensure proactive compliance and reduce the risk of non-compliance.

C. Preventing and resolving disputes with AI-based solutions

The integration of artificial intelligence (AI) in dispute prevention and resolution offers opportunities to effectively manage legal disputes related to audiobooks. This sub-chapter explores the different methods and techniques used to prevent and resolve disputes using AI.

1. Early detection of litigation risks

AI algorithms enable early detection of litigation risks by analyzing contracts, interactions and stakeholder behaviors. We'll dive into data analysis methods, anomaly detection models and early warning systems to identify red flags indicating potential litigation and take preventive action.

2. AI-assisted mediation and negotiation

AI offers advanced functionalities to facilitate mediation and negotiation between conflicting parties, proposing fair solutions and promoting constructive dialogue. We will look at preference modeling techniques, solution recommendation algorithms and collaborative learning systems to find acceptable compromises and avoid contentious disputes.

3. AI-assisted arbitration and adjudication

Finally, AI can assist arbitrators and judges in analyzing evidence, evaluating arguments and making informed decisions in legal disputes. We will explore legal text analysis methods, forensic prediction models and decision support systems to ensure fair and equitable decisions in dispute resolution.

STEP BY STEP IMPLEMENTATION: Rights management and legal compliance with AI

A. Use of AI tools to identify and verify copyrights and licenses required for audio production

When it comes to managing rights and legal compliance in audio content production, the application of artificial intelligence tools offers a revolutionary approach to simplifying and automating these complex processes. Here's a step-by-step method for harnessing AI in this area:

1. Understanding copyright issues

Before diving into the use of AI tools, it's crucial to understand the basics of copyright and licensing in the audio domain. Resources such as the SACEM and Creative Commons websites offer guides and training to familiarize you with these concepts.

2. Identification of Works and Rightsholders

Platforms such as Google's Content ID use AI to automatically identify copyrighted works by scanning uploaded content and comparing it with a database of registered works. For audio producers, the use of such systems ensures that any content incorporated into a production is correctly licensed.

3. Automated License Verification

Tools like Clarifai offer AI solutions capable of analyzing content and detecting specific elements, helping to verify whether the content licenses used match project requirements. By integrating these tools into your workflow, you can automate license verification and ensure project compliance.

4. Contract and License Management

AI can also simplify contract and license management with platforms like Contractbook or Icertis, which use AI to analyze, classify and manage legal documents. These systems can help track due dates, renewals and ensure that all audio productions comply with the agreements in place.

5. Training and Awareness

To take full advantage of these tools, invest in training and raising your team's awareness of the legal issues and capabilities of AI tools. Webinars, online courses on platforms like Coursera or edX, or audio industry-specific workshops can be valuable resources.

6. Technological and legal watch

Keep abreast of the latest technological advances and legal developments in copyright and licensing. Following specialized blogs, participating in professional forums and attending conferences can help you anticipate changes and adapt your practices accordingly.

By integrating AI into copyright and licensing management, audio content producers and creators can not only optimize their processes but also reinforce the legal compliance of their productions, reducing the risk of litigation and promoting serene creation that respects the works of others.

B. Set up automated processes to monitor and ensure compliance with local and international regulations

In the complex world of rights management and legal compliance, automating monitoring processes can play a key role. Here are some concrete steps and resources for implementing these processes:

1. Identifying regulatory requirements

Start with a comprehensive analysis of local and international regulations applicable to your audio content, including copyright, privacy standards such as RGPD in Europe, and other industry-specific legislation. Resources such as the WIPO (World Intellectual Property Organization) website can provide valuable information on international copyright.

2. Copyright monitoring tools

Integrate tools such as YouTube's Content ID, or similar systems developed by companies specializing in digital rights management (DRM), which automatically detect unauthorized use of copyrighted content. These systems compare works broadcast on platforms with a database of registered content to identify matches.

3. Automating RGPD compliance and other privacy regulations

Use platforms such as OneTrust or TrustArc, which offer solutions for automating compliance with privacy regulations. They enable you to carry out compliance audits, manage user consents and respond to requests for access to personal data.

4. Internal systems development

For specific needs not covered by existing tools, consider developing customized solutions. Using AI frameworks to analyze contracts, legal documents and content can help identify compliance risks. Python libraries such as spaCy or NLTK can be useful for natural language processing applied to legal documents.

5. Training and awareness-raising

Ensure that internal teams are trained in compliance tools and processes. Organize training sessions on the use of compliance monitoring and management platforms, as well as on the fundamentals of applicable regulations.

6. Ongoing regulatory watch

Compliance is not a static state, but a dynamic process requiring constant monitoring. Set up alerts and specialized newsletters, such as those offered by law firms specializing in intellectual property, to keep abreast of legislative developments.

7. Regular audits

Schedule regular compliance audits to evaluate and adjust existing processes. Automated auditing tools can simplify this task by providing periodic reports on compliance and identifying areas requiring adjustment.

By following these steps and leveraging the resources mentioned, you can establish robust processes for monitoring and regulatory compliance, minimizing legal risks and strengthening the protection of your audio content when using AI.

C. Strategies for resolving legal disputes and IP-related litigation with the assistance of AI-based solutions

The integration of artificial intelligence into rights management and legal compliance offers new avenues for resolving intellectual property disputes. Here are concrete strategies, along with examples of AI-based solutions, for effectively navigating these legal challenges:

1. Automated detection and analysis of infringements

Use AI tools like Lex Machina to monitor the web and identify unauthorized uses of copyrighted content. These systems can analyze large quantities of online data to pinpoint potential infringements, providing a solid basis for legal action or negotiation.

2. Originality verification tools

Platforms such as Copyscape and Grammarly Premium include advanced features for detecting plagiarism in written texts, helping creators and publishers to ensure the originality of their content before publication. AI enhances these tools by improving their ability to identify subtle matches and assess content uniqueness.

3. AI-based legal assistance

Services such as ROSS Intelligence employ AI to provide legal assistance, facilitating precedent-setting research and case preparation for IP-related disputes. These solutions save time and improve the efficiency of legal processes by providing rapid access to relevant information.

4. AI-assisted negotiation and conflict resolution

Tools like Smartsettle are designed to facilitate conflict resolution by using AI to propose fair solutions based on the parties' preferences. These systems can help find common ground without resorting to costly and time-consuming legal proceedings.

5. License and contract management

The use of AI-based platforms such as Seal Software automates contract and license management, ensuring that agreements comply with intellectual property laws and identifying potentially problematic clauses before they cause disputes.

6. Ongoing training and awareness-raising

Encourage the use of online courses and webinars, such as those offered by Coursera or edX, to keep abreast of the latest trends and technologies in intellectual property law and AI. A thorough understanding of these areas is crucial to anticipating and avoiding litigation.

By applying these strategies and harnessing the capabilities of AI-based solutions, professionals can not only resolve IP-related conflicts more effectively, but also prevent them from occurring in the first place, ensuring smoother, more secure copyright management in the digital world.

Chapter 7: Data analysis and continuous improvement

A. Performance tracking and audience feedback analysis with AI

The integration of artificial intelligence (AI) into performance monitoring and audience feedback analysis offers opportunities for continuous optimization of audiobooks based on listener preferences and reactions. This sub-chapter explores the different methods and techniques used to track performance and analyze audience feedback using AI.

1. Analysis of listening and behavioral data

AI algorithms analyze listener listening and behavior data to understand their preferences, listening habits and reactions to audio content. We'll dive into real-time data analysis methods, content recommendation models and audience segmentation techniques to identify significant trends and patterns in listener behavior.

2. Satisfaction and performance assessment

AI offers advanced features for assessing listener satisfaction and measuring audiobook performance according to specific criteria such as content quality, narration, and listener engagement. We'll look at sentiment analysis techniques, satisfaction prediction models and automatic quality assessment systems to provide valuable insights into the user experience and effectiveness of audio content.

3. Recommendations for improvement and optimization

Finally, AI can be used to make recommendations for improving and optimizing audiobooks based on insights gained from data analysis and audience feedback. We will explore personalized recommendation generation methods, content recommendation algorithms and continuous learning systems to propose adjustments and improvements that meet listeners' needs and expectations.

B. Dynamic adaptation of content based on listener feedback

The integration of artificial intelligence (AI) in the dynamic adaptation of content based on listener feedback offers opportunities for the continuous adjustment of audiobooks to meet the changing needs and preferences of the audience. This sub-chapter explores the different methods and techniques used to dynamically adapt content based on listener feedback using AI.

1. Analysis of audience feedback and identification of trends

AI algorithms analyze audience feedback, such as comments, ratings and suggestions, to identify trends and recurring patterns in listeners' preferences and expectations. We'll dive into text analysis methods, clustering techniques and trend detection models to extract relevant insights from audience feedback.

2. Personalization and content recommendations

AI offers advanced features for personalizing audiobook content based on individual listener feedback and insights gained from data analysis. We'll look at dynamic content recommendation techniques, listener profiling models and adaptive recommendation systems to offer personalized adaptations that match each listener's specific interests and preferences.

3. Automatic, iterative content adjustments

Finally, AI makes it possible to automatically adjust audiobook content in response to listener feedback, and to measure the impact of these adjustments on audience engagement and satisfaction. We will explore closed-loop machine learning methods, continuous optimization algorithms and A/B testing techniques to rapidly iterate and progressively improve content in response to listener feedback.

C. Strategic evolution driven by predictive analytics and AI insights

The integration of artificial intelligence (AI) into the strategic evolution of audiobooks, guided by predictive analytics and insights from data, offers opportunities to make informed strategic decisions for the future of audio production and distribution. This sub-chapter explores the different methods and techniques used to guide strategic evolution through AI.

1. Predictive analysis of market trends

AI algorithms can analyze historical and current audiobook market data to identify emerging trends and predict future developments. We'll dive into predictive modeling methods, market forecasting techniques and growth models to anticipate future opportunities and challenges in the audio industry.

2. Identifying opportunities for innovation and differentiation

AI offers advanced capabilities for identifying opportunities for innovation and differentiation in audiobook production and distribution, by analyzing the changing needs and preferences of the audience. We will cover market analysis techniques, product recommendation models and competitive intelligence systems to propose targeted innovation strategies that meet market demands.

3. Development of expansion and diversification strategies

Finally, AI enables the development of expansion and diversification strategies based on insights from data analysis and market forecasts. We will explore product portfolio optimization methods, scenario simulation models and multi-criteria decision-making techniques to evaluate strategic options and choose the most promising growth paths for audiobooks.

STEP BY STEP IMPLEMENTATION: Data analysis and continuous iteration

A. Collection and processing of audience data from distribution platforms and listener feedback

The first step in understanding and continuously improving the audio experience is the efficient collection and rigorous processing of audience data. There are two main strands to this approach: the exploitation of data provided by distribution platforms, and the analysis of direct feedback from listeners.

1. Data collection on distribution platforms

Audiobook distribution platforms such as Audible provide a wealth of valuable information on listener behavior. Key indicators include the number of downloads, retention rates, listening times, and many other metrics that provide a detailed picture of listening preferences and habits.

2. Analysis of listener feedback

Comments, ratings and other forms of direct feedback from listeners are also essential. This feedback provides a qualitative overview of the user experience, highlighting the strengths and areas for improvement of the proposed content.

The processing of this data relies on advanced analytical tools and, increasingly, on artificial intelligence to generate actionable insights. The aim is to gain an in-depth understanding of listeners' expectations in order to adjust content production, selection and recommendation, as well as to refine marketing and distribution strategies.

This iterative approach, fueled by up-to-date and accurate data, is essential to remain competitive in the dynamic world of audiobooks. It enables us not only to maximize the engagement of existing listeners, but also to attract new users by offering ever more captivating and personalized listening experiences.

B. Use of AI algorithms for predictive analysis of market trends and listener behavior

The use of artificial intelligence (AI) algorithms for predictive analysis of market trends and listener behavior represents a revolution in the audiobook industry. This approach makes it possible not only to understand current dynamics, but also to anticipate future developments, providing a solid basis for strategic decision-making.

1. Predictive analysis of market trends

AI algorithms analyze historical and current data to identify emerging trends, forecast changes in consumer preferences and detect growth opportunities. Relying on techniques such as machine learning and time series analysis, audiobook publishers can anticipate market demands and adjust their offering accordingly.

2. Understanding listener behavior

AI enables in-depth analysis of listener behavior, identifying listening patterns, analyzing feedback and segmenting the audience. This detailed understanding of user expectations and preferences helps personalize recommendations and improve engagement.

3. Content personalization and recommendation

Thanks to the insights obtained, AI algorithms facilitate the creation of sophisticated recommendation systems, capable of offering listeners highly personalized content. This personalization enhances the user experience and increases loyalty.

4. Innovation and product development

Predictive analytics inform decisions on new product development and content innovation. By identifying emerging trends and untapped market niches, publishers can launch pioneering initiatives and stand out in the marketplace.

In summary, the use of AI algorithms for predictive analysis of market trends and listener behavior is opening up new horizons for the audiobook industry. It not only enables content and marketing strategies to be optimized in real time, but also shapes the future of the sector by anticipating listeners' needs and desires.

C. Methods for dynamically adjusting content and distribution strategies based on the results of data analysis

In a constantly evolving ecosystem like audiobooks, the ability to adapt quickly to listener feedback and market trends is crucial. The integration of dynamic methods to adjust content and distribution strategies relies on the judicious use of collected data. Here's how:

1. Analysis of audience feedback and identification of trends

The starting point is to analyze user feedback, whether in the form of comments, ratings, or listening behavior. AI algorithms are able to detect patterns and trends in this data, making it possible to identify what resonates most with the audience.

2. Personalization and content recommendations

With the insights gained, it is possible to further personalize the recommendations made to listeners. AI can adjust content suggestions in real time, according to individual preferences, increasing user engagement and satisfaction.

3. Automatic, iterative content adjustments

AI tools can automatically modify existing content or guide the production of new content according to listeners' reactions and preferences. This capacity for continuous adjustment ensures that the offer remains relevant and attractive.

4. Optimizing distribution strategies

By analyzing the performance of different distribution platforms and listeners' consumption habits, AI can help optimize distribution channels. This includes adjusting marketing campaigns, selecting priority platforms for certain releases, and adapting pricing models.

5. A/B testing and loop feedback

The implementation of A/B tests enables us to evaluate the effectiveness of adjustments made, by comparing the performance of different versions of a content or distribution strategy. The results of these tests feed into a continuous improvement process, where every decision is guided by concrete data.

6. Decision-making based on predictive analysis

Finally, the use of predictive models makes it possible to anticipate future trends and adapt strategies accordingly. Whether introducing new genres, exploring new formats, or expanding into new markets, predictive analysis offers a valuable compass for navigating uncertainty.

These methods, leveraging the analytical and adaptive capabilities offered by AI, enable the creation of an audiobook ecosystem where content and distribution evolve in perfect harmony with listeners' expectations, guaranteeing a consistently enriching and engaging user experience.

It's up to you!

The creation and sale of an audiobook follows several key stages, from initial conception to final sales analysis. Here's a detailed practical guide to each phase.

A. Step 1: Preparation and planning

1. Content Design and Planning

- Use Google Docs, Libre Office or Microsoft Word to write and organize your content. These tools are standard for document creation and offer sharing and collaboration options.
- For authors wishing to integrate elements of artificial intelligence (AI) into content creation, services like OpenAI's GPT (with interfaces like ShortlyAI or Writesonic) can help generate ideas, outlines, or even parts of text. These tools often have free plans with usage limits or trial versions.

2. Adapting the Script for Audio

- Adapting a written text into a script for narration requires careful attention to the details that make the content engaging to listen to. Standard word-processing software can be used for this step.
- AI tools like Descript can help edit and refine your script, offering suggestions to make the text sound more natural to the ear. Descript offers a free version with limited functionality.

3. Narrator's voice selection

For authors considering the use of synthesized voice, tools such as Balabolka (free) or online platforms offer text-to-speech services of reasonable quality. More advanced AI tools such as Amazon Polly or Google Cloud Text-to-Speech offer very natural voices and are chargeable, but with a generally affordable cost, often based on the amount of text converted.

In short, the preparation and planning stage is crucial to the success of an audiobook. The judicious use of free or low-cost tools, as well as the potential integration of AI technologies, can greatly facilitate this phase, making content more engaging and simplifying the creation process.

B. Stage 2: Production

1. Narration

1) Self-narration
Use a quality microphone and Audacity, a free audio recording and editing program, to capture your narration.

2) Professional narrators
Professional narrators can be found on platforms such as ACX. Costs vary, but it is possible to share revenues rather than pay in advance.

2. Recording and editing

1) Audacity
Perfect for basic recording and editing, free of charge.

2) Descript

Offers advanced audio editing features and the ability to remove words or phrases by editing the transcribed text of the audio. Descript offers a limited free plan.

3. Post-production

1) Auphonic

An online tool that automates leveling, equalization and noise reduction. There's a free monthly quota that may suffice for smaller projects.

2) Izotope RX

For more advanced audio editing needs, Izotope RX is a professional choice, but it comes at a price. However, it offers unrivalled tools for cleaning up and restoring audio.

4. AI integration for storytelling

1) Google Cloud Text-to-Speech

Transforms text into natural speech. Google Cloud offers a free access level with usage limits.

2) Amazon Polly

Another text-to-speech service that can be used to create audiobook narrations with natural-sounding voices. Polly is not free, but offers a free layer.

These tools offer a professional approach to audiobook production, even for those on a limited budget. The key is to judiciously combine the use of free and paid tools according to the specific needs of your project.

C. Stage 3: Distribution

Step 3, audiobook distribution, involves choosing distribution platforms and preparing your audiobook to meet their specific requirements.

1. ACX (Audiobook Creation Exchange)

It's the most popular platform for distributing audiobooks on Audible, Amazon, and iTunes. ACX offers detailed guides for preparing your audiobook to the required standards. Distribution via ACX can be done under a revenue-sharing model or by paying in advance.

2. Findaway Voices

An alternative to ACX that offers wider distribution to additional platforms like Google Play, Kobo, and more. Findaway Voices offers flexibility in terms of pricing and royalties, but there may be upfront costs for distribution.

3. Google Play Books

For those wishing to sell directly on Google Play, you can upload your audiobook there. This requires your audiobook to meet certain technical specifications.

4. Bandcamp

Although mainly used for music, Bandcamp can also be used to sell audio books. This platform offers total control over pricing and a large share of revenues.

For AI tools in distribution, the focus is on sales optimization and analysis rather than distribution itself. Use analytical tools like Google Analytics to track traffic to your website or sales page and adjust your marketing efforts accordingly.

Each platform has its own requirements in terms of audio format, quality and metadata. Be sure to read their guidelines carefully before submitting your audiobook.

D. Stage 4: Marketing and Promotion

1. Cover design

Use Canva to create an attractive cover. Choose a template suited to your genre and personalize it with the title of your audiobook and your name. Canva is intuitive to use and comes with many free elements.

2. Social Media Strategy

Plan and schedule regular publications on your social networks with Hootsuite or Buffer. Share excerpts from your book, anecdotes about the creative process, and listener reviews to engage your audience.

3. Email Marketing

Create an email campaign with Mailchimp to announce the release of your audiobook to your mailing list. Include a direct link to purchase or listen, and consider offering a free chapter as an incentive.

4. Paid advertising

Launch targeted campaigns on Google Ads and Facebook Ads to reach potential listeners outside your network. Use relevant keywords and target according to interests related to your book genre.

5. Website or landing page creation

Build a website with WordPress or create a landing page with Squarespace to showcase your audiobook. Include a biography, reviews, purchase links, and a contact form.

6. Using AI for Promotional Content

Generate content ideas or write engaging descriptions with an AI tool like ChatGPT. This content can be used on your website, in your emails, or as scripts for promotional videos.

Each step should be tailored to your budget, target audience and sales objectives. Measure the effectiveness of your marketing efforts regularly to adjust your strategy as needed.

E. Stage 5: Sales and Analysis

1. Sales follow-up

Use the dashboards provided by distribution platforms (such as ACX or Findaway Voices) to track sales and downloads of your audiobook. These tools provide key data on sales performance.

2. Data analysis

Integrate Google Analytics into your website or sales page to gain insights into visitor behavior and the effectiveness of your marketing campaigns.

3. Adjustment of Marketing Strategy

Based on the data collected, adjust your marketing strategy. For example, if you notice that certain ads are generating more traffic, increase your budget in those channels.

4. Collecting Feedback

Encourage listeners to leave reviews on distribution platforms, and use their feedback to improve your product or marketing.

These actions will help you optimize your sales and refine your marketing strategy for future projects.

F. Summary

1. Preparation and Planning

1) *Audio Book Design*
Define content, target audience and format.

2) *Script adaptation*
If your content is not originally in audio format, adapt it for narration.

2. Production

1) *Narration*

Choose between narrating yourself or hiring a professional narrator. Platforms like ACX offer a wide choice of narrators.

2) *Recording and editing*

Use audio editing software such as Audacity (free) or Adobe Audition (paid) to record and edit your audiobook. Make sure you record in a quiet, echo-free environment.

3) *Post-production*

Clean up the audio to remove any background noise, ensure consistent volume levels and improve clarity. Tools like Izotope RX offer advanced features for audio enhancement.

3. Distribution

1) *Choosing a Platform*

Decide whether you want to distribute exclusively via a single platform like Audible (via ACX) for potentially higher royalties, or distribute widely across multiple platforms including Google Play Books, Kobo, etc., for a broader reach.

2) *Format and Qualitative Verification*

Make sure your audiobook meets the technical specifications of your chosen distribution platforms. ACX, for example, has specific requirements in terms of bit rate, noise floor, and so on.

4. Marketing and Promotion

1) *Cover Design*

Create an attractive cover that matches the theme and genre of your audiobook. Canva offers both free and premium design templates.

2) *Marketing strategy*

Use social networks, email marketing and other digital marketing strategies to promote your audiobook. Consider creating a website or landing page for your book.

3) *Notice and Launch*

Encourage early listeners to leave reviews. Plan a launch strategy that could include discounts, gifts or promotional exchanges with other authors.

5. Sales and Analysis

1) *Sales follow-up*

Use the analysis tools provided by your distribution platforms to monitor sales. This data will help you better understand your audience and adapt your future marketing efforts.

2) *Strategy adjustment*

Based on sales data and listener feedback, adjust your marketing strategy and consider updates to your audio content or promotional tactics.

6. Tools & Resources

1) *Narrating and recording*
ACX, Audacity, Adobe Audition

2) *Edition*
Izotope RX, Auphonic (for equalization and noise reduction)

3) *Cover Design*
Canva, Adobe Spark

4) *Distribution*
ACX (for Audible and iTunes), Findaway Voices (for wide distribution)

5) *Marketing*
Social networking platforms, Mailchimp (for email marketing), WordPress or Squarespace (to create a promotional website)

Creating and selling an audiobook is a journey that requires creativity, marketing skills and a willingness to adapt based on listener feedback and sales performance.

Made in United States
Troutdale, OR
03/21/2024

18643013R00056